SSI MONOGRAPH

CHINA-LATIN AMERICA MILITARY ENGAGEMENT: GOOD WILL, GOOD BUSINESS, AND STRATEGIC POSITION

R. Evan Ellis

August 2011

*****

Comments pertaining to this report are invited and should be forwarded to: Director, Strategic Studies Institute, U.S. Army War College, 632 Wright Ave, Carlisle, PA 17013-5046.

*****

All Strategic Studies Institute (SSI) publications may be downloaded free of charge from the SSI website. Hard copies of this report may also be obtained free of charge while supplies last by placing an order on the SSI website. The SSI website address is: *www.StrategicStudiesInstitute.army.mil*.

*****

The Strategic Studies Institute publishes a monthly e-mail newsletter to update the national security community on the research of our analysts, recent and forthcoming publications, and upcoming conferences sponsored by the Institute. Each newsletter also provides a strategic commentary by one of our research analysts. If you are interested in receiving this newsletter, please subscribe on the SSI website at *www.StrategicStudiesInstitute. army.mil/newsletter/*.

FOREWORD

The reemergence of China on the global stage is arguably one of the most important phenomena of our time. With its sustained high rates of economic growth, the People's Republic of China (PRC) has dramatically increased trade and investment flows with the rest of the world, including regions such as Latin America, with which it historically has had very little interaction. In many of these countries, the PRC has gone from having an almost negligible economic presence to replacing the United States as the number one or number two trading partner. Moreover, particularly since the end of the global financial crisis, Chinese companies, in coordination with the Chinese government and banks, have begun to make multibillion dollar loans and investments in Latin America, creating a rapidly expanding presence of Chinese companies and workers in the region in such sectors as construction, logistics, manufacturing, telecommunications, and retail. In terms of "soft power," the PRC has arguably captured the imaginations of Latin American political leaders, businessmen, and students as a power meriting attention and, in some cases, courtship.

While a great deal of attention has been given to Chinese commercial activity in Latin America, very little has been written in the open press regarding Chinese military engagement with the region. While visits by senior military leaders and major arms sales are reported in the Latin American press, there has been, to date, almost no detailed, comparative analysis of the PRC-Latin America military relationship. This is particularly striking, given the emphasis placed on military relationships in determining whether Chinese engagement with the region constitutes a threat to U.S. national security interests.

Dr. Evan Ellis of the Center for Hemispheric Defense Studies fills an important void in the burgeoning literature regarding China's activities with Latin America. This monograph provides a detailed, region-wide analysis of PRC military engagement with Latin America, including not only arms sales, but also senior-level military visits, personnel exchanges, and activities of the People's Liberation Army (PLA) in the region, ranging from its 6-year participation in the United Nations (UN) peacekeeping forces in Haiti, to its November 2010 humanitarian exercise in Peru, *Angel de la Paz*. The work leverages the extensive Spanish and English-language primary research by Dr. Ellis in the open source literature of the region, as well as off-the-record interviews with current and former Latin American military officers who have directly participated in the activities treated.

Dr. Ellis explains that Chinese military activity in Latin America is far more extensive than is commonly recognized. At the same time, it also goes against conventional wisdom by arguing that, in the short term, such activity does not seek to achieve formal alliances or a permanent military presence in the region, but rather to advance commercial and political objectives to include increasing China's understanding of, and influence within, Latin American governments.

While the arguments of Dr. Ellis may be surprising to some, the monograph will undoubtedly serve as an important reference point for scholars from multiple perspectives: those following the rise of China, those studying Latin American security issues, students of international relations, and students of U.S. national security, among others.

In the course of these expanding interactions, the PRC has emphasized the "peaceful nature" of its interactions, which have profound implications not only for the world's economy, but for its security environment as well. The growth of China has played out differently in each region.

DOUGLAS C. LOVELACE, JR.
Director
Strategic Studies Institute

ABOUT THE AUTHOR

R. EVAN ELLIS is a professor of national security studies, modeling, gaming, and simulation with the Center for Hemispheric Defense Studies, with a research focus on Latin America's relationships with external actors, including China, Russia, and Iran. His work in this area includes the 2009 book, *China in Latin America: The Whats and Wherefores*, and over 20 articles in English and Spanish published over the past 6 years in magazines and journals ranging from *Joint Forces Quarterly* to *Air and Space Power Journal* en Espanol to the *Revista de Dinámica de Sistemas*. Dr. Ellis has presented his work in a broad range of business and government forums in Argentina, Belize, Bolivia, Brazil, Canada, Chile, Colombia, Dominican Republic, Ecuador, El Salvador, France, Jamaica, Mexico, Norway, Panama, Paraguay, Peru, the United Kingdom, the United States, Uruguay, and Venezuela. He is a frequent guest lecturer at the U.S. Air Force Special Operations School. Dr. Ellis holds a Ph.D. in political science with a specialization in comparative politics.

SUMMARY

Over the past several years, the People's Republic of China (PRC) has expanded its military ties with Latin America in multiple important ways. High-level trips by Latin American defense and security personnel to the PRC and visits by their Chinese counterparts have become commonplace. The volume and sophistication of Chinese arms sold to the region has increased. Officer exchange programs, institutional visits, and other lower-level ties have also expanded. Chinese military personnel have begun participating in operations in the region in a modest, yet symbolically important manner.

Military engagement among Western countries traditionally has focused on securing greater capability for confronting an adversary, including alliances and base access agreements, that confer strategic geographical position. By contrast, Chinese military engagement primarily supports broader objectives of national development and regime survival. This includes building good will, understanding, and political leverage among important commercial partners and technology sources, creating the tools to protect PRC interests in countries where it does business, selling Chinese products and moving up the value-added chain in strategically important sectors, and positioning the PRC strategically, even while avoiding alarming the United States over its activities in the region.

Chinese military engagement with the region may be understood in terms of five interrelated types of activities: (1) meetings between senior military officials, (2) lower-level military-to-military interactions, (3) military sales, (4) military-relevant commercial interactions, and (5) Chinese physical presence within Latin America with military-strategic implications.

Based on official visits documented in the press, the number of visits by senior Chinese defense officials to Latin America, and visits by their counterparts to China, has increased over the past several years. In the second half of 2010, the number of contacts was particularly high, including nine visits at the Minister of Defense or Chief of Staff level between senior Chinese military officials and their Latin American counterparts, in Venezuela, Ecuador, Chile, Mexico, Brazil, Colombia, Peru, and Bolivia.

The PRC has expanded the quantity and scope of its military-to-military contacts at the institutional level, including its ongoing participation in the peacekeeping mission in Haiti and an increasing number of personnel exchanges for training and education, joint exercises, institutional visits, and symbolic activities. Chinese institutions host Latin American military personnel from at least 18 states in Latin America in a range of Chinese People's Liberation Army (PLA) institutions including the PLA Defense Studies Institute in Changping; the Army Command College and the Chinese Navy Command School, both in the vicinity of Nanjing; and a facility in Shijiazhuang. In November 2010, the PLA also conducted its first bilateral military exercise in the region, the humanitarian assistance exercise *Angel de la Paz*.

In the domain of military sales, Chinese activities in Latin America are also much more extensive than is generally recognized. Although such sales were once impeded by concerns over quality, maintenance, and logistics support, Chinese arms conglomerates such as NORINCO are moving up the value-added chain, leveraging the opening provided by Venezuelan purchases of K-8 aircraft and JYL-1 radars, selling similar equipment to Venezuelan allies Ecuador and Bolivia, and proving their goods in the region in general. Other landmark purchases include the lease of MA-60 transport aircraft to Bolivia, with a sale of 4 of the same aircraft under negotiation with Ecuador, as well as the sale of WMZ-551 armored personnel carriers to Argentina, and the subsequently cancelled sale of MBT-2000 main battle tanks to Peru. Training of military personnel, as well as command and control packages such as that by Huawei for the Venezuelan organization DICOFAN, have also been important, as has the donation of nonlethal goods. Bolivia stands out for the quantities of trucks, busses, and other goods donated to the Bolivian military by the PLA since 2006, as does Jamaica, whose very small defense force received a $3.5 million donation of nonlethal goods in the months following the exposure of serious capability gaps associated with its forced entry into the Tivoli Gardens neighborhood.

In addition to arms sales and contacts between the PLA and Latin American militaries, select commercial interactions must be considered as part of its military engagement. In Latin America, this includes collaboration between the Brazilian aircraft manufacturer Embraer and China Aviation Industrial Corporation (CAIC) II to produce ERJ-145s business jets in Harbin, China, as well as sales of Y-12 turboprop aircraft to Venezuela. In the space industry, ties include four major ongoing space-related projects in Latin America, the China-Brazil Earth Research Satellite (CBERS), Venesat-1, the Venezuela Remote Sensing Satellite, and the Tupac Katari satellite, as well as other projects in development and more modest collaboration initiatives. In the telecommunications industry, Chinese firms such as Huawei and ZTE are major players in the leading nations of Central and South America.

Finally, China has a low-profile but important physical military presence in Latin America , including military police in Haiti since September 2004, as well as a reported presence in at least three Soviet-era monitoring facilities: Lourdes, Bejucal,[1] and Santiago de Cuba.[2] In addition, the presence of Chinese logistics companies in major ports of the region could facilitate operations by the PRC in the region should relations between the United States and the PRC significantly worsen in the coming decades.

In analyzing the implications of the Chinese military presence in the region, this author recognizes that such presence can contribute to legitimate regional security needs, but also foment misunderstanding. It argues that the United States should work with China to achieve greater transparency regarding those activities, and to engage the PRC in a positive fashion regarding their activities in the hemisphere, including regular dialogue and the establishment of mechanisms for resolving misunderstanding. In addition, however, it must improve its understanding of the specific dangers and threats that could flow out of this presence, using methodologies such as scenario-based gaming, to see how different actors in the region could seek to leverage or be influenced in their actions by the presence of China, including indirect pressures, and how the commercial and other interests in Latin America of actors such as Russia, Iran, and India might play into the unfolding dynamic.

ENDNOTES - SUMMARY

1. Manuel Cereijo, "Inside Bejucal Base in Cuba: A Real Threat," *The Americano*, August 27, 2010, available from *theamericano.com/2010/08/27/bejucal-base-cuba-real-threat/*. Cereijo's allegations concerning Bejucal, however, have been questioned by Cuba scholar William Ratliff, among others, noting that the radar domes in the photo accompanying Cereijo's article are not located at Bejucal, as represented, but rather at the U.S.-operated Menwith Hill facility in the United Kingdom. See "Cereijo, Bejucal, China and Cuba's adversary foreign intelligence (Bill Ratliff, U.S.)," Stanford, CA: World Association of International Studies, April 3, 2006, available from *waisworld.org/go.jsp?id=02a0&objectType=post&objectTypeId=3776&topicId=10*.

2. "Chinese Signals Intelligence and Cyberwarfare in Cuba," *AFIO Weekly Intelligence Notes*, No. 23-06, June 12, 2006, available from *www.afio.com/sections/wins/2006/2006-23.html#ChinaInCuba*.

CHINA–LATIN AMERICA MILITARY ENGAGEMENT: GOOD WILL, GOOD BUSINESS, AND STRATEGIC POSITION

INTRODUCTION

One of the most common statements made in discussions of Chinese engagement with Latin America is that such ties are primarily "commercial" in nature. While true, the focus on the commercial dimension of the relationship conceals the fact that, over the past several years, the People's Republic of China (PRC) has also expanded its military ties with Latin America in multiple important ways, consistent with its own public declarations of intention. In November 2008, for example, the PRC issued its first official policy paper on Latin America in which it announced that it sought to enhance "mutual visits by defense and military officials of the two sides as well as personnel exchanges," and to deepen "professional exchanges in military training, personnel training and peacekeeping."[1]

China's military engagement with Latin America in recent years has both expanded and deepened in a quite public manner. High-level trips by Latin American defense and security personnel to the PRC and visits by their Chinese counterparts have become commonplace. The volume and sophistication of Chinese arms sold to the region have increased. Officer exchange programs, institutional visits, and other lower-level ties have also expanded. Chinese military personnel have begun participating in operations in the region in modest, yet symbolically important ways.

1

Since the granting of port concessions in Panama to the Hong-Kong-based firm Hutchison Whampoa in 1999, Chinese military engagement with Latin America has been one of the most broadly discussed, but misunderstood, dimensions of PRC activities in the region.[2] The PRC's military initiatives in Latin America are arguably not the largest or most strategically significant part of its rapidly expanding interactions with the region. Nor do they visibly threaten the United States or undermine pro-Western regimes in the same fashion as Soviet military engagement with Latin America during the Cold War. The initiatives, however, are significant and growing, and continue to be a key to the evaluation by U.S. decisionmakers as to whether the Chinese presence in Latin America constitutes a strategic threat to U.S. interests.

The purpose of this monograph is to analyze PRC defense and security ties in Latin America. While it also touches upon commercial and scientific activities that may have military relevance, its focus is on activities in the military and police sphere, which have not, to date, been analyzed in detail in a single document. The monograph is divided into three sections:

1. Objectives of PRC defense and security engagement with Latin America,

2. Manifestations of that engagement, and

3. Conclusions.

OBJECTIVES OF PRC DEFENSE AND SECURITY ENGAGEMENT WITH LATIN AMERICA

Given the predominantly commercial nature of Chinese interactions with Latin America, it is important to begin the analysis of PRC military activities in the region with a discussion of Chinese motivations for engagement with Latin America in general, and how military ties and transactions simultaneously support and put at risk those goals.

While the PRC has publicly professed its interest in expanding military linkages with Latin America, it has given very little explanation of its reasons for doing so, or how its military activities fit into its broader engagement with the region. This does not imply that such motivations are inherently nefarious — only that they must be examined, based on the available evidence as well as current and historical patterns of Chinese decisionmaking.

In the spirit of Chinese thinkers such as Sun Zi, PRC military initiatives in Latin America should be understood as subordinate to, and in support of, long-term PRC national objectives in the region. In general, these objectives involve promoting and protecting China's reemergence as a major global actor. The imperatives and risks involved are a product of the export-led growth strategy that the PRC has pursued and refined since 1978. Specifically, it has leveraged the opportunities presented by global information and trade flows, and its initial comparative advantage in abundant inexpensive labor to serve as a global manufacturing hub, attracting and using foreign investment in a deliberate fashion to build its physical and technological infrastructure and diversify its economic base, and thus moving progressively into ever higher value-added economic activities.[3]

China's pursuit of this strategy, and the nation's place in the global economy, has created a number of imperatives:

1. securing access to reliable sources of primary products in support of manufacturing activities and capital formation,

2. assuring the ability to feed the Chinese population as it both urbanizes and consumes more protein,

3. establishing and protecting markets for Chinese goods as its producers continue to expand production and move up the value-added chain,

4. securing access to technology and global information flows,

5. maintaining a presence in institutions key to China's global economic transactions, and

6. avoiding the consolidation of an international coalition opposing the "rise" of the PRC.

Chinese military engagement with Latin America supports each of these imperatives, albeit often in indirect ways. Chinese President Hu Jintao addressed the role of the Chinese military in support of national development objectives in his call for the Chinese People's Liberation Army (PLA) to carry out its "new mission in the new century."[4] Similarly, China's *2006 National Defense White Paper* refers to the role of the PLA in "fostering a security environment conducive to China's peaceful development."[5] Similar language is contained in the November 2007 constitution of the Chinese Communist Party, and the *2008 National Defense White Paper.*[6] Chinese authors have written about the new "interest frontier" of the PRC, suggesting that the PLA has an obligation to defend not only Chinese interests within the physical territory of the PRC, but to protect those interests which are found outside it as well.[7]

Because U.S. political leaders generally view military activities in a manner very distinct from trade and investment, Chinese leaders have incentives to be quite cautious in their military engagement to avoid undermining important national strategic goals in Latin America. As a result, the imperatives for the

PRC of military engagement in Latin America contrast sharply with conventional wisdom regarding the use of the military instrument. These imperatives may be inferred as follows:

1. Building good will, understanding, and political leverage,

2. Creating the tools to protect PRC interests in-country,

3. Selling Chinese products and moving up the value-added chain,

4. Positioning the PRC strategically in the region, and

5. Reassuring the United States.

Building Good Will, Understanding, and Political Leverage.

For the PRC, military engagement is one tool among many for building political good will and leverage in a country to make more likely that it will not oppose the entry of Chinese products or act against its investments. Military activities are useful in this context because the armed forces remain an important political actor in most Latin American countries, although thinking of the military as a political instrument is also consistent with both Chinese communist and pre-communist philosophy.

Knowing and being on good terms with the military leadership of a Latin American country help the Chinese to understand the overall political dynamic of that country, anticipate actions that could be taken against PRC commercial interests, influence the political leadership through military friends where necessary, and anticipate or avoid actions that could be taken by the armed forces in the political arena that could impact Chinese interests.

Within the larger framework of military engagement, people-oriented activities such as leadership visits, training, and exchange programs are particularly useful because they allow the PRC to confer personal benefits and establish relationships with current and future defense leaders, while avoiding the type of symbolism that military bases or military end-item sales generate for Western analysts.

Creating the Tools to Protect Chinese Interests In-Country.

As Chinese companies and businessmen expand their physical presence in Latin America, they will experience a corresponding increase in the security challenges to people and operations that have confronted the companies of other countries operating in the region, including kidnapping, extortion, and violence associated with strikes, political protest, and terrorism. Chinese petroleum and mining firms operating in remote areas are particularly vulnerable, as seen by violence against Andes Petroleum and Petroriental north of Ecuador in 2006[8] and 2007.[9] Problems may also be expected with the transportation of goods on newly opened highways and rail routes over the Andes and through the Amazon jungle, such as the northern and southern "bioceanic corridors" crossing Peru, the "interoceanic corridor" from the north of Chile through Bolivia and Brazil, and the future Manta-Manaus corridor.[10] Cultural differences between the Chinese and local populations are also likely to contribute to tensions and increase the possibilities for violence, as seen in the 2007 truckers' strike against Chinese shopkeepers in Buenos Aires, Argentina,[11] or the November 2004 violence against Chinese communities in Maracay and Valencia, Venezuela.[12]

In the near term, PRC companies will have to rely upon Latin American police and armed forces, as well as private security and the payment of protection money, in order to avoid harm to Chinese personnel and operations. As the value of Chinese investments in the region and the resources flowing from it grow, the PRC will have an increasing incentive to improve the functionality of these security forces, and to ensure that the protection of Chinese personnel and operations receives priority. Similarly, it will have incentives to become involved in issues of port and airport security in the region, as well as high-value geography which impacts the movement of goods, such as the Panama Canal, as well as highway, rail, and alternative canal routes crossing the continent.[13]

Indeed, the PRC has already demonstrated a willingness to use its military to protect its commercial interests in Africa, citing threats to these interests as justification for deploying naval forces to conduct anti-piracy operations in the Gulf of Aden in December 2008.[14] Also, there is already an ongoing debate within the PRC regarding the best ways to protect Chinese commercial operations, including discussions by retiring PLA military officers to form private security companies to support commercial ventures abroad.[15]

Selling Chinese Products and Moving Up the Value-Added Chain.

Although Chinese military exports are relatively small by comparison to other goods, they contribute to PRC national development in multiple ways. As with other commercial products, military products generate export revenues for Chinese companies such as the defense conglomerate NORINCO, and sustain employment. Sales of nonlethal military goods such as clothing and personal equipment in Latin America by Chinese companies, for example, are often overlooked, but are a nontrivial business. Such sales also sustain the health of the PRC defense industrial base, and help it to advance its technical capabilities in support of national defense goals. This is particularly the case with respect to high-end goods such as radars, aircraft, armored vehicles, and other sophisticated military end items or "dual-use" commercial goods, where sales in Latin America help China to test, prove, and refine its capabilities under field conditions in strategically important sectors.

Positioning China Strategically in the Region.

Chinese military thinkers, as others around the world, recognize the implications of the emergence of the PRC as a principal global actor, including the need to prepare for large-scale hostilities to protect these global interests. Although the PLA is very careful to cast its military preparations as "defensive" in nature, debates within the PLA over the need to develop a "deterrent force," and references to an "active defense"[16] implicitly acknowledge that Chinese thinkers have contemplated the necessity of carrying a future conflict to the adversary. Moreover, although the PRC currently lacks the capability to project significant military capability beyond Asia, the pursuit of "defense in depth" by the PLA Navy foresees conducting the battle as far away from its shores as capabilities will allow, while references in the *2008 Defense White Paper* to close coordination between military struggle and political, economic, and diplomatic endeavors[17] suggest a global approach to thinking about warfare.

Nothing in the public discourse of the Chinese leadership, policy papers, or debates suggests that Latin America is considered in the short term as a base for military operations. Nonetheless, in the long term, when the PRC is both economically and militarily more powerful than it is today, the ability to deter a strategic adversary such as the United States through holding it at risk in its own theater, and to disrupt its ability to project power at home before those forces can reach the PRC, is consistent with the aforementioned concepts, including a holistic, asymmetric approach towards warfare.[18]

Within this broad approach, China's military ties in Latin America afford geographically-specific benefits, such as collecting intelligence on the operation of U.S. forces, creating diversionary crises, closing down strategic chokepoints such as the Panama Canal, or conducting disruption operations in close proximity to the United States.

Reassuring the United States.

As noted previously, the PRC's pursuit of military objectives in the region is subordinate to its broader national objectives. Where the two conflict, the exact balance will reflect the perceptions and self-confidence of the Chinese leadership and its propensity for risk-taking, factors which continue to evolve with each successive generation of Chinese leadership. Direct forms of security assistance, for example, may support the objective of protecting Chinese companies and resource flows, yet undermine the more important strategic objective of preserving access by the PRC to Western technology and markets. At the very least, China has strong incentives to portray all military interactions with Latin American states in a way that avoids an appearance of threatening the United States, so as to minimize the risk of damage to its broader objectives. In many cases, this goal not only will impact how China represents its activities, but how it structures them. Gifts of military medical capabilities or logistics gear, for example, may be preferable to selling or donating more lethal end items because the former generates similar institutional good will and contacts, while appearing less threatening.

In general, as this section has suggested, the course taken by Chinese military engagement with Latin America in the medium or long term is likely to differ significantly from that witnessed with respect to Soviet military activities in the region during the Cold War. In general, the PRC is more likely to refrain from overtly provocative activities, such as the establishment of bases with a significant Chinese presence, overt military assistance to groups trying to overthrow a regime, unilateral military intervention in the region in a contested leadership situation, or participation in anti-US military alliances.

MANIFESTATIONS OF CHINESE MILITARY ENGAGEMENT WITH LATIN AMERICA

Chinese military engagement with the region may be understood in terms of five interrelated types of activities: (1) meetings between senior military officials, (2) lower-level military-to-military interactions, (3) military sales, (4) military-relevant commercial interactions, and (5) Chinese physical presence within Latin America with military-strategic implications.

Meetings Between Senior Military Officials.

Based on official visits documented in the press, the number of visits by senior Chinese defense officials to Latin America, and visits by their counterparts to China, has increased over the past several years. The press accounts of the agendas of these visits suggest that the purpose is often to establish or strengthen relationships, including not only exchanging views on security matters, but also to discussing or finalizing agreements for arms purchases, military exchanges, or other contacts and transactions.

In the second half of 2010, the number of high-level military-to-military contacts was particularly high, including eight clusters of visits at the Minister of Defense or Chief of Staff level between senior Chinese military officials and their Latin American counterparts, including Venezuela, Ecuador, Chile, Mexico, Brazil, Colombia, Peru, and Bolivia.

1. In August 2010, Bolivian minister of Defense Ruben Saavedra traveled to the PRC to meet with his counterpart, then Chinese Minister of Defense Cao Gangchuan.[19]

2. In September, Cuban General Leopoldo Cintra Frias traveled to Beijing to meet with Minister Cao and other senior PRC defense leaders.[20]

3. Later the same month, Chief of the PLA General Staff Chen Bingde traveled to Lima, Peru, for a visit that included a joint military-humanitarian exercise between Chinese and Peruvian armed forces and the donation of a $1.3 million mobile field hospital to the Peruvian Army.[21]

4. Also in September, the new Chinese Minister of Defense, Liang Guanglie, traveled to Bogota, Colombia, on the first of a three-nation visit to Latin America,

meeting with Colombian Defense Minister Rodrigo Rivera and other senior Colombian officials, and signing a defense cooperation agreement. [22]

5. Following his visit to Colombia, Minister Liang traveled to Brasilia, where he met with Brazilian Defense Minister Nelson Jobim,[23] reciprocating a visit paid by Jobim to China at the beginning of the same month.[24]

6. The third leg of the September 2010 trip by Minister Liang took him to Mexico, where he met with the senior leadership of both of the institutions of the Mexican armed forces: The Ministry of National Defense (SEDENA) and the Ministry of the Navy (SEMAR).[25]

7. In November 2010, Chief of Staff Chen traveled to Quito, Ecuador, on the first stop of a two-nation visit, meeting with the Ecuadoran Minister of Defense Javier Ponce, as well as the head of Ecuador's Joint Chief of Staff, Luis Ernesto Gonzalez.[26]

8. In the second stop of his trip, General Chen traveled to Caracas, Venezuela, where he met with his counterpart, Defense Minister Carlos Figueroa, to prepare the military portion of the agenda for the 9th annual ministerial-level meeting of the "China-Venezuela High-Level Mixed Commission," held in Beijing during the subsequent month.[27]

Although little of the substance of the discussions during these visits makes it into the open press, their role in advancing military relationships between China and the Latin American counterpart nation has arguably been greater than is generally recognized: such visits allow the leaders involved to build familiarity and confidence by speaking face-to-face, and to explore possibilities for future projects, from arms sales to expanded military exchanges. Such visits also gen-

erally include tours of host nation facilities and opportunities for informal discussion, raising possibilities for collaboration on issues which have captured
the attention of the leaders involved, within the limits
of their national policies. In some cases, initiatives
prepared prior to the trip by staff officers or other officials are ratified during the high-level visit, while
ideas generated during discussions become initiatives
to be subsequently explored, administratively driven
by the declared interest of the senior leadership.

Lower-Level Military-to-Military Interactions.

In the past several years, the PRC has expanded the
quantity and scope of its military-to-military contacts
at the institutional level, including its ongoing participation in the peacekeeping mission in Haiti and an increasing number of personnel exchanges for training
and education, joint exercises, institutional visits, and
symbolic activities. In each of these, the primary value
for the PRC is arguably building relationships at the
institutional level, as well as at the personal level with
future key figures in Latin American militaries. In the
process, it has also been able to increase its understanding of Latin American militaries and the security
environment of the region.

In Haiti, military police from the PLA continue to
serve as part of the United Nations peacekeeping force
(MINUSTAH) present in the country. Chinese peacekeepers have had a continual presence in Haiti since
the first contingent was deployed in September 2004.
Haiti also has the dubious distinction of having been
the site of the first officially-recognized Chinese military casualties on Latin American soil. Eight members
of the PLA were among the personnel killed in Haiti

in January 2010, in conjunction with the earthquake that devastated the country.[28] Four of the Chinese killed were members of the MINUSTAH police force, while the other four were part of a six-person working group from the Ministry of Public Security which was visiting the United Nations (UN) headquarters facility when its roof collapsed due to the earthquake.[29] The bodies of the victims were subsequently returned to the PRC, where they posthumously received various honors.[30]

The participation of the Chinese military in MINUSTAH for more than 6 years has arguably yielded great benefits for the PRC. It has given the PLA and hundreds of its soldiers first-hand experience in operating in the Latin American environment in a police and security role—something which will be of particular value in the future if China begins to provide security assistance to allies in the region in support of the protection of its nationals and ongoing operations. In addition, its presence in MINUSTAH has allowed the PLA to better understand and build relationships with the militaries of Brazil and other nations working alongside it in the operation, even while fostering good will in the region toward the PRC as a contributor to the international order. Finally, the Chinese presence in Haiti has also arguably advanced its campaign to isolate Taiwan internationally, since it puts pressure on the government of Haiti, which currently affords diplomatic recognition to Taiwan, rather than the PRC.[31]

In the realm of training and military education, Chinese institutions host Latin American military personnel from at least 18 states in Latin America—virtually every country in the region with which the PRC has diplomatic relations. The examples listed in the following paragraphs are merely illustrative:

The National Defense University of the PLA has multiple institutions offering courses in both English and Spanish to Latin American officers. These include:

1. The Defense Studies Institute in Changping (near Beijing), a school especially for foreigners within the broader university, offering courses in both Spanish and English, including the following:

- A 5-month senior staff course, taught primarily in Spanish. The course is presented by a combination of Chinese instructors and Communist-party vetted translators. Latin American nations sending officers have included Mexico, Peru, Chile, Colombia, and Uruguay. The Chilean army has been sending officers to the course since 1999, while the Uruguayans have been sending students since at least March 2009.
- A 3-month course on strategy, campaign planning, and military thinking, attended by officers of the Chilean Navy, among others, since 1997.
- A 10-month course on "national defense and command," taught in English and attended by officers from the Peruvian Army, the Chilean Navy and Air Force, and the Uruguayan Navy and Air Force, among others.[32]
- A 5-month course on Military Strategy, taught in Spanish, and attended by Peruvian Army officers and Chilean Air Force personnel, among others.

2. The Army Command College, located in Nanjing, offers a 4-month course in English and French, which has been attended by military officers from Latin American countries including Colombia, Peru,

Barbados, and Jamaica, as well as Africa and other regions.

3. The Chinese Navy Command School, outside of Nanjing, offers a 1-year senior command course in English. The course has been attended by Latin American military officers, among others, including officers from Uruguay[33] and Brazil.[34]

4. In a facility near Shijiazhuang:
- A 5-month course on special forces operations at the tactical-operational level. It has been attended by officers from Uruguay for at least the past 2 years, and perhaps by members from other armed forces.
- A 5-month infantry company course, attended by an officer from Uruguay in 2010, and perhaps others.

5. The Center of Military Instruction of the PLA offers a course on martial arts which has been attended by Chilean Marines, among others.

Other Chinese military institutes which have hosted students from Latin American countries include the following:

1. The Naval Research Institute, near Beijing, which hosted a low-ranking officer from the Uruguayan Navy and perhaps others for a "masters" course in naval radar and sonar, during an 11-month stay in Beijing from 2008-09.

2. An institute in Beijing hosted two low-ranking officers from the Uruguayan Air Force and perhaps others during an 11-month stay in the city from 2008 to 2009:
- One for a "masters" course on aerial communication.
- One for a course on artillery repair.

In parallel with these programs, Latin American militaries also hosted Chinese officers. Examples include the following:

1. For several years, beginning in 2005, the Chilean Army language school hosted two Chinese professors for the Mandarin Chinese language,[35] although as of January 2011, these instructors were no longer present.

2. In 2006, during a visit by a delegation from the Chinese National Defense University, the Chilean war college ANEPE signed an agreement regarding officer exchanges and collaborative activities, although it has not yet been ratified.

Chinese collaboration with Latin American militaries on education and training is increasingly extending to tactical-level programs as well. During the November 2010 meeting between Chinese Defense Minister Liang Guanglie and Colombian Defense Minister Rodrigo Rivera, an expansion of Sino-Colombian military exchanges was agreed to, including the establishment of 10 places for Colombian generals and colonels in Chinese military academies, and the sending of Colombian trainers to China for courses in sharpshooting, combat under-water diving, survival, and riverine combat.[36] Similarly, during General Liang's September meeting with Brazilian Defense Minister Nelson Jobim, expanded cooperation between the two countries in the area of basic training was discussed.[37]

In addition to opportunities for building personal relationships and gathering intelligence, such tactical-level courses also help the PRC to develop military capabilities in areas which may be useful in working more directly in the region's unique operating environments.

An additional element of China's forming of military relationships with Latin America is institutional visits. Such visits typically involve more people, but are much shorter in duration than training exchanges. Although the opportunities to develop personal ties are by necessity more superficial, such institutional visits allow the PRC to reach larger groups of personnel whose work touches many others, such as military professors and mid-grade officers, while also building or strengthening institution-to-institution linkages. Examples include the following:

- Visits between Chinese and Chilean naval officers have occurred on an occasional basis since July 1996, but increased to one or two per year starting in 2005.
- In Argentina, there has been a similar increase in recent years, including visits by Chinese officials to the Argentine National Defense University and the senior war colleges.
- In Colombia, delegations from China's National Defense University visit the nation's war college on an annual basis.

Beyond institutional visits, other ongoing contacts between Chinese and Latin American militaries include port visits by military training ships and warships by each side. The first such visit was made by the Chilean Navy training ship *Esmeralda* to the port of Shanghai in 1972. By 2009, the *Esmeralda* had made 10 trips to Chinese ports. Reciprocally, in April 1997, the first Chinese naval flotilla visited Latin America. It included the missile destroyers *Harbin* and *Zhuhai* and the logistics ship *Nancang*, which made port calls in Mexico, Peru, and Chile, as well as the U.S. base at Pearl Harbor.[38] The most recent such visit, at the time of this writing, came in 2009 from a Chinese naval flotilla which included the destroyer *Shijiazhuang* and the supply ship *Hongzehu*, making port calls in Valparaiso, Chile; Callao, Peru; and Guayaquil, Ecuador.[39] Benign in character, such visits benefit the PLA Navy, helping it to identify requirements for the use of Latin American ports by its ships in the future for maintenance, resupply, or other purposes.[40]

In addition to bilateral contacts, such as those mentioned above, Chinese and Latin American militaries have occasional contact through conferences and other forums. The Chilean and Chinese navies, for example, have regular contact through the Western Pacific Naval Symposium, with the PRC having supported Chile's admission to the organization.[41] The Chinese, for their part, host various forums to which Latin American officers are invited, including an annual "symposium for upper level officers" in Beijing, which has been held at least five times. In addition, from November to December 2007 in the city of Qingdao, the headquarters of the PLA North Sea fleet, the Chinese held a seminar on the management of search and rescue operations in which a Uruguayan naval lieutenant and perhaps other Latin American military officers were present.

It is also important to mention Chinese military actions in Latin America which are important primarily at the symbolic level. These include one on September 16, 2010, when an honor guard of 34 persons from the PLA participated, alongside representatives from 15 other countries, in a parade in Mexico City in commemoration of the 200th Anniversary of Mexico's independence from Spain.[42]

Finally, military-to-military contacts also have come to include joint exercises. In November 2010,[39]

Chinese military personnel participated with 50 Peruvians in the humanitarian exercise *Angel de la Paz*, including deployment to the village of Villa Maria del Trunfo to perform medical services for the local population.[43] The joint exercise simulated a response by the two armed forces to an earthquake, with an associated chemical fire,[44] and was tied to the donation by the PLA to the Peruvian military of a mobile field hospital and training of the recipients on its use in the facilities of the 1st Special Forces Brigade in Chorrillos, near Lima.[45]

While not threatening in and of itself, Chinese participation in a humanitarian exercise in Latin America may be understood as a logical step toward its participation in the response to an actual disaster, outside the framework of a multilateral force such as the UN. Such an offer of direct military involvement in a Latin American country would put U.S. policymakers in an awkward position, since publicly blocking humanitarian assistance from the PRC could be construed as increasing the number of Latin American deaths from the disaster in order to keep the Chinese military "out of the U.S. backyard." The U.S. response to future PRC offers of direct military humanitarian assistance should thus be considered carefully by U.S. policymakers before they occur.

Military Sales to Latin America.

As with military sales by other countries, Chinese military sales to Latin America help the PRC to strengthen its ties with the purchasers by meeting their specific needs, and by tying those nations logistically to Chinese maintenance and training infrastructures. Such transactions also help the PRC to develop and sustain its own national defense industry, and earn export sales revenues.

Innocent or not, Chinese arms sales to Latin America are arguably one of the most closely watched facets of China's engagement with Latin America. Although U.S. leaders such as Assistant Secretary of Defense Frank Mora have observed that Chinese arms sales can contribute to security in the hemisphere,[46] many politicians and other policymakers look at such sales as indications that Chinese activities in the region constitute a threat to U.S. national security.

In general, PRC military sales to Latin America have followed the pattern of its commercial sales. The first Chinese defense goods sold in the region were relatively inexpensive, unsophisticated items such as military clothing and personal equipment. In some cases, such goods entered Latin American militaries as donations, such as the annual $1 million dollars worth of hats, gloves, and other nonlethal equipment donated by the PLA to Colombia. Frequently, Chinese goods have been offered by third party importers, representing companies such as the China North Industries Corporation (NORINCO) in the PRC, but licensed to do business with Latin American militaries.

As with commercial goods, China's ability to sell sophisticated military hardware to Latin America has been impeded by concerns over quality, as well as the difficulty of maintaining and supporting the equipment. Such concerns have been particularly acute with respect to materiel such as ships, aircraft, armored vehicles, weapons, and communication systems, regarding which lives on the battlefield could depend on the proper functioning of the equipment. The lack of a Chinese military presence in the region has compounded such concern; the absence of sales of Chinese gear in Latin America meant that Chinese military goods were "unproven" in the region, and thus more difficult to sell. Moreover, without a Chinese military presence in the region, maintenance and obtaining spare parts for Chinese goods were, in the minds of many leaders, a great risk.[47]

Despite such obstacles, as in the commercial realm, with time, the PRC and its defense companies have begun to move up the value-added chain to sell increasingly sophisticated military goods in Latin America. In doing so, it has exploited opportunities provided by regimes hostile to the United States, such as Venezuela, Ecuador, and Bolivia, whose political orientation and inability to acquire Western military technology have led them to look to Chinese equipment.

The first major breakthrough for the PRC in making military sales to Latin America was arguably Venezuela's 2008 announcement that it would purchase K-8 (Karakorum) aircraft, co-developed with Pakistan.[48] Venezuela's decision to purchase the aircraft was driven in part by its inability to purchase U.S. fighters, or spare parts for its existing fleet of U.S. aircraft, as well as successful U.S. efforts to block other Western countries from selling to Venezuela similar aircraft that incorporated U.S. technology.[49] The agreement to ultimately purchase a total of 18 K-8 aircraft from China National Aero-Technology Import and Export Corporation (CATIC), along with armaments and a supporting logistics package, was made in August 2008. In the second half of 2009, 11 Venezuelan pilots and 56 technicians were sent to China for training on the aircraft as pilots and maintenance and logistics support staff.[50]

The first 6 K-8s were officially received in March 2010,[51] with the other 12 arriving in August. They were assigned to the 12th Fighter Air Group, based at the air base *Rafael Urdaneta de Maracaibo*, and to the 15th Special Operations group, at the air base *Vicente Landaeta Gil de Barquisimeto*.[52] As a result of Venezuelan satisfaction with the transaction, the number of K-8s desired was expanded to 40. In addition, the Venezuelan military leadership has been evaluating the more capable Chinese L-15 *Air King*, with a proposal by Hongdu Aviation Industry Corporation to sell the Venezuelans 24 of the aircraft.[53]

Despite highly positive statements by the Venezuelan leadership regarding the K-8s, and the increase of the purchase to 40 aircraft, the acquisition has had its problems. In January 2010, one of the K-8s piloted by a newly trained Venezuelan crashed on takeoff at the military airport in Barquismetro, near Caracas.[54] While the Chinese blamed improper maintenance by the recently trained Venezuelans, the Venezuelans pointed the finger at the Chinese for poor translations of the aircraft technical manuals into Spanish. Beyond fighters, the government has also declared that it will purchase 10-12 Y-8 Chinese medium military transport aircraft, each capable of carrying up to 88 persons or 20 tons of cargo.[55]

With the support of President Hugo Chavez, purchases of Chinese equipment by the Venezuelan armed forces also expanded into other areas. In 2005 the Venezuelan air force acquired JYL-1 radars, usable for air defense, from the firm China National Electronics Import and Export Corporation (CEIEC), at a cost of $150 million.[56] The radars were acquired by the Venezuelan organization Compañía Anónima Venezolana de Industrias Militares (CAVIM), with the first delivered in January 2008 and subsequently put under the command of the Venezuelan Air Force. They were used publicly for the first time in 2008 in an exercise with Brazil.[57]

The Chinese also installed a command and control center for the Venezuelan radars at a military base near Caracas at the end of 2008. Between April and August 2008, Venezuela sent a total of 70 officers to the PRC for training on the operation and maintenance of the system.[58] By mid-2009, the Venezuelan military leadership was referring to a total of 10 Chinese radars as being operational.[59] Moreover, as of June 2009, Venezuela was evaluating the purchase of other Chinese radars to complement the capabilities of the JYL-1s.[60]

In addition to the radars and aircraft, the Venezuelans have also spearheaded the introduction of Chinese command and control equipment into Latin America, with the Venezuelan defense organization DICOFAN working with the Chinese civilian telecommunications firm Huawei to implement the system.[61] In support of the system, China has funded a training program executed by Huawei for students of the Venezuelan military institute *Universidad Nacional Experimental Politécnica de las Fuerzas Armadas* (UNEFA),[62] as well as construction of a $54 million laboratory in the Venezuelan Armed forces technical university *Instituto Universitario Militar de Comunicaciones y Electrónicas de las Fuerzas Armadas* (IUMCOELFA).

Despite press accounts which suggest that Chinese military sales in Latin America have been relatively limited, by the end of 2010, the Venezuelan military leadership was evaluating purchase of a broad range of Chinese systems, including such command and control systems as high frequency (HF), ultra high frequency (UHF), and very high frequency (VHF) communications systems; IGLA missile systems; antiaircraft guns; biodegradable mines; water purification equipment; bridging equipment; utility aircraft; anti-submarine aircraft; ground-attack aircraft; long-range sea surveillance aircraft; costal patrol aircraft; frigates; submarines; and anti-submarine warfare (ASW) helicopters.

Beyond purchases of PRC military hardware, Venezuelan officials have also reportedly facilitated indirect purchases of military goods by criminal and insurgent groups such as the *Fuerzas Armadas Revolucionarias de Colombia* (FARC). An investigation by the Colombian prosecutor's office, for example, implicated the Venezuelan government official Amílcar Figueroa, who presented a shopping list of weapons for the FARC during his visit to the weapons manufacturer NORINCO in the PRC.[63]

In addition to direct purchases of military goods and systems from the PRC, Venezuela has greatly facilitated the ability by the PRC to sell its military end items to other, like-minded governments in the region, including both Ecuador and Bolivia. Following the lead of Venezuela, in September 2009 Ecuador negotiated a deal with the PRC for two radars, manufactured by China Electronics Technology Corporation (CETC), to be deployed to its northern frontier with Colombia for evaluation, with the option to purchase an additional four units.[64] Although there were problems with the suitability of the first radars for the operating conditions they encountered, in August 2010 the Ecuadoran government announced that it was going ahead with the purchase of the four additional radars, at a cost of $80 million, and would begin taking delivery on them by the end of the year.[65]

In addition to the radars, Ecuador has acquired MA-60 medium transport aircraft from the PRC. The first two aircraft acquisitions were in 2006.[66] Ecuador continues to flirt with the purchase of more Chinese mid-sized transport aircraft. In July 2009, Ecuadoran Defense Minister Javier Ponce noted Ecuadoran interest in purchasing four military aircraft from the PRC for $60 million to replace its aging fleet of Brazilian *Avro* military transport aircraft.[67] Although no purchases immediately followed the declarations, during the February 2010 visit to China by Chairman of the Ecuadoran Joint Chiefs of Staff General Fabian Varela, the PRC mentioned that it was investigating the possibility of providing Ecuador with four MA-60s[68] at a price of $80 million.[69] Subsequently, in August 2010, Ponce announced that he was sending a delegation to the PRC to negotiate the purchase of two of the MA-60s for $38 million, to be delivered by the end of the year,[70] although there have been no further reports in the press on the status of the transaction.

In addition to these transactions, the PRC has donated military trucks and ambulances and other non-lethal goods to Ecuador. Indeed, during the February 2010 visit by General Varela to the PRC, China announced that it planned to double such donations.[71]

Like Ecuador, Bolivia has followed the lead of Venezuela in acquiring military equipment from the PRC. Prompted in part by the personal recommendation of Venezuelan President Hugo Chavez to his colleague Evo Morales in October 2009, Bolivian Defense Minister Walker San Miguel announced the planned purchase of a squadron (6) of Chinese K-8 aircraft for $58 million.[72] The aircraft are to be deployed in the vicinity of Cochabamba for counterdrug interception missions, and represent the first combat aircraft acquired by the Bolivian military.[73] The deal was financed with a 25-year concessional credit, with the aircraft to be delivered over the course of 18 months beginning in April 2010.[74]

Although the K-8s are Bolivia's first fighters, they are Bolivia's second transaction with the PRC involving aircraft for its military. In March 2007, Bolivia announced the leasing of two MA-60 military cargo and passenger aircraft from the PRC, as part of a larger deal that included the acquisition of military transport aircraft from Venezuela.[75] The Chinese MA-60 aircraft were paid for by a $38.3 million loan from the PRC[76] and delivered in February 2008.

In addition to its purchase of end-items, Bolivia has also received a series of donations of other military goods from the PRC. These donations have come in four major installments: In December 2006, the PRC announced the donation to Bolivia of 25-person assault craft, infantry and artillery munitions, night-vision goggles, and kevlar helmets.[77] In 2007, the Bolivian armed forces received 34 trucks from the manufacturer First Auto Works (FAW), five busses, three Toyota Land Cruiser SUVs, and a tow truck.[78] In February 2009, it received 2 gunboats from the PRC.[79] In March 2010, it received 27 busses for military transport, manufactured by the Chinese company Hinger, 21 Nissan light trucks, and 40 Yamaha outboard motors.[80] Beyond these items, over the period 1987-96, the PRC also reportedly provided 10,000 AK-47 assault rifles,[81] in addition to having donated motorcycles, bicycles, and other gear to the Bolivian police.

Although the most significant arms transactions between the PRC and Latin America have come in the "socialist" countries of the Bolivarian Alliance for the Americas (ALBA) bloc—Venezuela, Cuba, Nicaragua, Bolivia, Honduras, Dominica, Ecuador, plus a few small island nations—significant advances and near-advances have occurred in other countries as well. In 2009, Peru almost became the first nation in

Latin America to make a major purchase of armored vehicles from the PRC. A series of five Chinese MBT-2000 tanks were accepted from the PRC for evaluation by the Peruvian army, and were featured prominently in a military parade in December 2009.[82] The purchase came under significant criticism within Peru, and was eventually canceled by the Minister of Defense in the interest of dedicating more resources to fighting narcotraffickers and recouping the state presence in the Apurimac and Ene valley region (VRAE) in the interior of the country.[83]

As noted previously, in 2010 Peru was also the recipient of the first major donation of military humanitarian equipment from the PLA, with the delivery of a mobile field hospital and other equipment during the second half of 2010, having a total value of $300 million, including training of Peruvian personnel on the equipment, and culminating in a joint Chinese-Peruvian humanitarian exercise in November of that year. At a lower level, Peru has also purchased Chinese nonlethal equipment, and in 2007 signed defense accords with the Chinese to allow them to participate more directly in the Peruvian military acquisition system.[84]

However, Peru has not been the only U.S. ally in the region to consider major purchases of Chinese military equipment. Since as early as 2006, Chinese military officials have discussed the possibility of selling armored vehicles and other equipment to the Colombian military.[85] To date, Colombia has not pursued such transactions, in part due to concern over complications in the maintenance and support of such equipment, and also because of the close Colombia-U.S. defense and security relationship.

Beyond explicit military sales, the Uruguayan police, the Peruvian National Police (PNP), and perhaps other police forces in the region have explored purchases of Chinese equipment. The police force in Montevideo, for example, has purchased police cruisers of the Chinese brand, Geeley.[86] Similarly, in August 2007 the PNP contracted with a South Korean intermediary for the purchase of 700 Geeley police cars.[87] As with the military sales, however, the transaction came under significant public scrutiny and was eventually canceled.

At a lower level, the Colombian military has also been the recipient of approximately $1 million per year of nonlethal equipment, including gloves and winter hats to equip Colombian high-mountain battalions. It affirmed and deepened that relationship in November 2010 with the signing of a defense cooperation accord.[88]

Costa Rica is also a strong candidate for the receipt of Chinese equipment and other assistance for its security forces. In November 2010, during a visit to Beijing, Costa Rican Prime Minister Rene Castro made a formal request to China for assistance in training and equipping its national police for operations against narcotrafficking.[89]

Other countries in the region have also flirted with the possibility of acquiring significant military material from the Chinese. These include Argentina, which in 2007 was reportedly considering purchase of the Chinese X-11 helicopter[90] as well as military trucks and radars to provide coverage for the Northern frontier.[91] It ultimately decided not to purchase any of these from the PRC.

The Argentine military did, however, agree to purchase WMZ-551 wheeled armored vehicles from the

Chinese manufacturer NORINCO as part of its contribution of a mechanized battalion to the joint Argentine-Chilean peacekeeping force "Cruz del Sur." In 2008, the Argentine Joint Staff purchased four of the armored vehicles for evaluation at a price of $2.6 million, including a training and spare parts package.[92] The vehicles initially saw service with the Argentine mechanized battalion in Gonaives, Haiti, where the Argentine combined mechanized battalion was deployed as part of MINUSTAH.[93] In the end, however, numerous problems with these vehicles led Argentina to suspend their procurement.[94]

In the case of Brazil, which has its own well-developed defense industry, there have been no significant purchases of Chinese military hardware. Nonetheless, the possibility of China-Brazil co-production of such items was discussed during the September 2010 meeting between Chinese Defense Minister Liang Guanglie and his Brazilian counterpart, Nelson Jobim, in Brasilia.[95]

Although Chile has made significant military purchases in general, it has not, to date, made significant purchases of Chinese military goods. As with Colombia, this resistance reflects Chile's close military institutional ties with the United States, including an existing military infrastructure built around U.S. and European equipment, as well as a relative emphasis on quality, over price—a luxury permitted in part thanks to its large military acquisition budget, which receives 10 percent of export revenues from the state mining firm *Corporación Nacional del Cobre de Chile* (COLDELCO), per the 1976 Copper Reserves Law.[96]

Finally, PRC donations of military equipment to Jamaica in January 2011 deserve mention. The delivery of $3.5 million in nonlethal goods, principally uniforms and tents, but also including helmets, binoculars, backpacks, and bulletproof vests to the Jamaica Defense Force (JDF) was based on a 2008 defense cooperation agreement between the two countries.[97] Although the donation was small in absolute terms, and did not involve weapon platforms or sophisticated munitions, it is significant because of the small size of the JDF, and because it came at a time in which the overtaxed Jamaican security forces were evaluating new ways of dealing with narco-violence such as that which killed 73 persons during the forced entry into Tivoli Gardens to capture Dudus Coke in May 2010. Such gifts, in combination with Chinese experience in neighboring Haiti, potentially position the PRC to expand its role in police-related activities among those nations that recognize the PRC in the Caribbean.

There have also been some suggestions that Chinese small arms have made their way into the arsenals of Latin American countries. For example, a version of the Colt M-4 rifle, manufactured by the Chinese arms conglomerate NORINCO as the CQ-M4, was reportedly spotted in 2008 photos of activities by the Paraguayan armed forces.[98]

Chinese military sales to non-state actors in the region also deserve mention. In addition to the previously discussed sale of Chinese arms to the FARC and other anti-governmental groups, a significant portion of the military-caliber weapons purchased by narcotrafficking organizations in Mexico are Chinese in origin, albeit purchased through third-party arms dealers.[99]

Military-Relevant Commercial Interactions in Latin America.

In addition to arms sales and contacts between the PLA and Latin American militaries, select commercial interactions must be considered as part of its military engagement because of the impact they confer upon Chinese military capabilities and its strategic posture globally. Although virtually all commercial interactions indirectly contribute to the resources and technological capability of the Chinese state, this section focuses on three strategic commercial areas whose military benefits are most explicit: aircraft, satellites, and telecommunications.

Chinese sales of aircraft to Latin America, as well as collaboration in aircraft manufacturing, benefit the Chinese military aviation industry. Both major cases of their collaboration involve the group Aviation Industry of China (AVIC), a holding company for CAIC I and II, also involved in the development of military aircraft and associated technology.

In the Brazilian case, CAIC collaborated with the Brazilian aircraft manufacturing firm Embraer to jointly manufacture the mid-sized ERJ-145 jet in the Chinese city of Harbin. Embraer viewed collaboration with CAIC as necessary in order to gain access to the Chinese market, although by 2010 the relationship had broken down, with the PRC resisting Embraer requests to move beyond the ERJ-145s and sell the larger E-190 to the Chinese market.[100] The relationship was also soured by the perception within Embraer that the Chinese had used the partnership to steal Embraer's technology to support their own aircraft development initiatives.

In the case of Venezuela, in April 2010, the two governments signed an agreement for the establishment of a new mid-sized airline to serve rural Venezuela.[101] China Development Bank agreed to lend the Venezuelan government $300 million to establish a regional airline. In return, the Venezuelan government would purchase the 33 aircraft for the airline, Y-12s, from AVIC.[102]

Satellites and space technology are other areas whose technology has both significant commercial and military applications for the PRC. Today, concurrent with the economic and technological development of the PRC, the Chinese space program is pursuing a diverse array of objectives, ranging from commercial satellite launches, to manned space flight (Project 921),[103] to missions to the moon,[104] Mars, and beyond.

Within this broader context, the PRC is attempting to secure a presence in the commercial satellite market. Under the supervision of China National Space Agency (CNSA), space launches and related activities are executed by the state-owned enterprise China Aerospace and Technology Corporation, with a series of companies falling within this framework. These include Great Wall Industry Corporation (GWIC), the sole organization authorized by the Chinese Government to provide satellite in-orbit delivery (IOD) services, commercial launch services, and aerospace technology applications.[105]

The PRC currently has four major ongoing space-related projects in Latin America: the China-Brazil Earth Research Satellite (CBERS); Venesat-1; the Venezuelan Remote Sensing Satellite (VRSS); and the Tupac Katari satellite, as well as other projects in development and more modest collaborative initiatives.

The primary venue for China-Brazil space cooperation is the China-Brazil Earth Resources Satellite program, established in 1998. To date, a total of three satellites have been launched through the program from the Taiyuan Satellite Launch Center in Shanxi, China, in 1999, 2003, and 2007.[106] A fourth launch is scheduled in mid-2011.[107] Brazil assumed approximately 30 percent of the project cost, while China assumed the remaining 70 percent, including ground stations.[108] The importance of the project in the broader Brazil-China relationship is evidenced by the fact that a key stop during President Hu's visit to Brazil in November 2004 was to a CBERS project site at the National Institute for Space Research (INPE) in the state of Sao Paulo.[109]

The China-Brazil space collaboration via the CBERS program has not been without problems. The launch of the first joint satellite, originally scheduled for 1992, was delayed until 1998.[110] Moreover, in August 2003, the first CBERS satellite experienced a malfunction that put an end to all of its data transmissions, and in April 2005 one of two PRC-supplied imaging devices on the second CBERS satellite stopped working due to a power supply failure.[111]

Such difficulties have not, however, significantly impeded China-Brazil space cooperation.[112] Upon assuming his post in March 2008, the new head of the Brazilian Space Agency stated that Brazil cherished its ties with the PRC and would deepen its cooperation with China in the field of space technology.[113] In the cases of Venezuela and Bolivia, the PRC has contracted to develop and launch satellites, to build associated ground control stations, and to train personnel in their use.

Venezuela was the first country in Latin America to pay a Chinese company, GWIC, to develop and launch a satellite.[114] Venezuela paid the PRC $406 million for the project, including $241 million to develop and put it into space.[115] As part of the project, the Chinese also built a series of ground control stations, including facilities at Camatagua and El Sombrero (the "Manuel Rios" military base). In addition, 90 Venezuelans were sent to the PRC for education and training associated with the project, including 15 technicians sent for a 12-month doctoral-level program, and an additional 15 sent for a shorter program to obtain their master's degrees.

The satellite was launched from the PRC in October 2008 and put into a 78-degree geosynchronous orbit, becoming operational in January 2009.[116] It initially had problems due to an irregular orbit, requiring adjustments from booster rockets that ultimately consumed a significant percentage of its operational life. Venezuela has discussed plans to launch a second satellite in 2013, the VRSS, which would conduct reconnaissance.[117]

In the case of Bolivia, on April 2, 2010, the government of Evo Morales contracted with the Chinese Aerospace Science and Technology Corporation (CASC) for the development and launch of the Tupac Katari satellite.[118] As in the Venezuelan case, the Bolivian project also included the construction of ground control stations: one in Pampahasi and one in La Guardia in the department of Santa Cruz.[119] Of the total $295 million cost of the program, all but $44 million was financed by credit from the China Development Bank.[120]

In addition to their contributions to the enhancement of the PRC space capability, China's construction of ground control stations and tying them into national telecommunication networks gives it unprecedented opportunities to understand the communication and space-technical architectures of each host country, and to tap into them in the future, if necessary, to collect information or disrupt them. In the case of Venezuela, it is relevant that the Chinese telecommunication company Huawei plays an intimate role not only in the construction of the satellite command and control facility, but also in the construction of the Venezuelan fiber optic network.[121]

From a military perspective, the utility of projects such as those with Brazil, Venezuela, and Bolivia, is that they help major Chinese companies in their bid to become a commercially viable space launch and technology provider, in competition with established providers such as Ariane and Thales. Moreover, associated training of Latin American personnel in the PRC arguably provides China the opportunity to build relationships with, collect information from, and in some degree indoctrinate virtually the entire cadre of the recipient country's military and civilian space-technical personnel.

As part of the development of its space sector, the PRC has also been pursuing initiatives in Argentina, Chile, and Peru, albeit with mixed success. With respect to Argentina, in May 2005 the Chinese government signed an agreement to provide technical support and equipment to the national satellite manufacturer *Investigaciones Aplicadas* (INVAP) in support of the development of a satellite by the Argentine national company *Empresa Argentina de Soluciones Satelitales* (ARSAT).[122] In the end, however, Astrium and Thales Alenia Space, rather than the PRC, were selected as the major equipment suppliers to INVAP. Moreover, although the PRC was interested in providing Argentina with launch services, ARSAT contracted with the French firm Arianespace to launch the satellite in mid-2012 from the equatorial launch site in New Guinea.[123]

In the case of Chile, China expressed an interest in participating in the development and launch of Chile's first satellite, the *Sistema Satelital de Observación de la Tierra* (SSOT).[124] But when the final decision was made, the development work was awarded to the European firm EADS Astrium,[125] and the launch contract won by Arianespace.

In the case of Peru, the nation is currently the only Latin American member of the Asia-Pacific Space Cooperation Organization (APSCO), a Beijing-based entity which began functioning in 2008, focusing on space science and technology, training, and cooperative research.[126]

In Mexico, the April 2010 legislation establishing a Mexican Space Agency[127] opened a window for China-Mexico space cooperation, with a delegation from the China National Space Agency participating in the new organization's kickoff event, the "Space Conference of the Americas," held in November 2010 in the Mexican state of Hidalgo.[128]

With respect to telecommunications, another sector with strategic value in the information operations and defense technology realm, Chinese firms are major players in virtually every major nation in Central and South America. The principal companies involved are Huawei, ZTE Corporation, and to a lesser extent Shanghai Alcatel Bell. Both Huawei and ZTE have established regional hubs for operations and training in Brazil. Both have participated in various projects in the modernization and expansion of major South American telecommunications architectures, including those of Brazil, Argentina, Chile, and Venezuela.[129]

In the cases of both Huawei and ZTE, Venezuela presented the companies, and the PRC, with a major commercial opportunity, with each establishing a cell phone manufacturing facility in the country, with plans to export production from the factories into other parts of the region.[130] In addition, Huawei has played a major role in building Venezuela's fiber optic network, and has been involved in a series of military projects as noted earlier, such as the establishment of a command and control facility, and the training of Venezuelan military personnel.

In the case of Shanghai Alcatel Bell, the company is the principal contractor laying a new fiber optic cable tying Cuba and Jamaica into the China-built Venezuela telecommunications infrastructure.[131] In Honduras, although the nation does not diplomatically recognize the PRC, a Chinese consortium was reportedly interested in purchasing the state telecommunications firm *Empresa Hondureña de Telecomunicaciones* (Hondutel), pursuant to plans to privatize it.[132]

As in aviation and space, Chinese activities in telecommunications have strategic military implications in two areas. First, they support Chinese efforts to acquire and improve technical capabilities in this strategically important sector. Second, as a complement to space cooperation, when Chinese companies sell hardware and build the telecommunications infrastructure in a region, the PRC is afforded opportunities to exploit these networks for future information collection and disruption activities in the unlikely but possible event of a future conflict with the United States. Moreover, such a presence makes possible the use of commercial telecommunication offices and activities as cover for the potential introduction of personnel into the region and performance of information operations.

Chinese Physical Presence within Latin America with Military-Strategic Implications.

To date, the PRC has been extremely cautious to avoid establishing an overt military presence in Latin America that could facilitate the emergence of a consensus within the United States and its allies to oppose PRC engagement with the region. Where it has done so, it has maintained a very low profile, or emphasized the scientific or nonmilitary character of that presence.

As noted previously, the PRC has had military police in Haiti as part of the MINUSTAH peacekeeping force since September 2004.[133] Such participation has arguably provided a valuable learning experience and engagement opportunity for them. While far more benign than other forms of presence, such as military bases, its activities in Haiti allows the PRC to gain experience and develop contacts in the region, while fostering good will among Latin American militaries that could facilitate its military access to the region in the future.

In Cuba, the PRC reportedly has a physical presence at three or more Soviet-era monitoring facilities: Lourdes, Bejucal,[134] and Santiago de Cuba.[135] With their proximity to the United States, the bases are reportedly used by the Chinese for the collection of signals intelligence, such as intercepting radio and cellphone transmissions, and also for the operation of a cyber espionage and training facility in the country.

In addition to their explicitly military presence in Haiti and Cuba, the PRC also has a series of government-operated scientific bases in Antarctica, since establishing its first base there, "Great Wall," in 1985.[136] Although the sites are not of a military character, they are supported by the PLA Navy, with the 1st Task

Group established in 2004 for the specific purpose of supporting the base and conducting operations in the "southern ocean."[137] Although the frigid temperatures and remoteness of its Antarctic facilities from the majority of Latin American states limit their military utility, as with Haiti they have provided opportunities to interact with the Argentine and Chilean militaries. The Chilean base in Antarctica, for example, is located in close physical proximity to that of the Chinese, providing opportunities for communication and collaboration. In addition, some have speculated that the PRC presence in Antarctica may strengthen its claim to exploit mineral deposits there,[138] particularly when the current international treaty banning mining in Antarctica expires in 2048.[139]

Beyond Haiti, Cuba, and Antarctica, the presence of Chinese logistics companies in major ports of the region arguably has some strategic military value, presenting a platform from which the PRC could smuggle people or material into the region under the cover of commercial operations, in the event that relations between the United States and the PRC significantly worsen in the coming decades. Indeed, there is a precedent for the use of Chinese commercial shipping for military purposes. In 1991, the PRC enlisted the help of the commercial cargo ship *Yongmen*, owned by China Overseas Shipping Company (COSCO), to evacuate Chinese embassy personnel from Somalia.[140]

While it is important to acknowledge the long-term strategic military value of the PRC physical presence in Latin America, it is also necessary to put it in proper context. It would be very difficult for the PLA to employ this commercial presence to support its own projection of military power in the region, since commercial facilities cannot be readily transformed into military bases. Moreover, the proximity to the United States of any improvised military facilities would make them highly vulnerable to military action in the event of overt hostilities. Nonetheless, in such a worst case scenario, such a presence would arguably allow the PRC to more easily deny the use of those facilities in the future by U.S. and allied warships, or to disrupt commercial flows that support the United States. The possibility that the firm Hutchison-Whampoa could use its port operations at Cristobal and Balboa in the Panama Canal Zone to close the canal to U.S. warships is illustrative.[141]

CONCLUSIONS

The PRC military relationship with Latin America is not as insignificant as much of the current discourse suggests, yet the challenges that it presents are often mischaracterized as a "China threat" to the region. From a U.S. national security perspective, the most important dimensions of China's military engagement with Latin America have to do with how the relationship is evolving as the PRC pursues its arguably legitimate national security interests, while remaining attentive to the United States, the most important strategic actor in the region. Chinese military interactions with Latin America, in and of themselves, are not necessarily a problem. The risk stems from what happens when the PRC, like the United States, is confronted with imperatives to protect its growing interests in the region in the face of organized crime or political turmoil that threaten its people, investments in Latin America, or commercial flows. Obviously, such disruption could in the future cause serious damage to the

Chinese economy. Equally troubling is how Chinese capital and weaponry could be used by regimes in the region hostile to their neighbors and the United States, or by terrorist groups and transnational criminal organizations. The principal risk is that such groups might acquire such weapons due to inadequate controls over them by the region's governments, or because of inadequate attention by Chinese companies regarding their weapons' ultimate customers. Chinese arms sales and the PRC physical presence in Latin America also become problematic in the event that U.S.-China relations degenerate, creating the paradox that U.S. fears over how such weapons and ties could be used would contribute to the very friction that could increase the possibility of their use.

Aside from such scenarios, even in the best of cases growing China-Latin America military engagement means that the United States will find its freedom of action in the region constrained in ways that were not the case in the past. Latin America is increasingly acquiring options beyond those offered by the United States, particularly as regarding its security cooperation, arms purchases, and personnel training. This dynamic will change how the region's governments bargain when it comes to access to bases, intelligence sharing, joint operations, and permission for U.S. direct action in the region, for example, counterdrug and counterterrorism operations. At a minimum, Latin American regimes will be more likely to resist agreeing to U.S. requests that are perceived to violate their sovereignty.

Based on its behavior to date, it is likely that the PRC will continue to expand its military engagement with Latin America, including arms sales, which will increase in volume and sophistication, building on the demonstration of its equipment in the ALBA countries, capitalizing on key breakthrough transactions when they occur—whether with Peru and Colombia, or elsewhere—in order to introduce end items into the mainstream arms market of the region. In following this course, although the PRC will likely remain highly attentive to the U.S. response, it is also likely to become bolder over time, particularly as the current 4th generation Chinese leadership is superseded by younger leaders who have grown up in a PRC that is an accepted political and economic power, confident of its place in the world.

What Should the United States Do?

Growing Chinese military contacts with Latin America are, in some ways, an understandable part of the expansion of the PRC as key global actor with global interests. Although the example of Japan suggests that a country that builds its economic power on international commerce in the modern era does not *necessarily* have to develop security ties with its trading partners, China seems bent on developing such ties.

As a long-standing military partner of Latin America, the United States has an opportunity to forge a new type of partnership with countries of the region, to help them exploit the opportunities and avoid the pitfalls that military and other forms of engagement with the PRC present. Indeed, as an integral part of the region through geographic, economic, and human ties, the United States has an *obligation* to itself and to its neighbors in Latin America to forge this new type of partnership.

Because of the importance of the United States for the PRC as a source of technology and as a market, and because of the damage that animosity with the United States could do to the economic and technological development of the PRC, Chinese leaders have traditionally been very sensitive to possible adverse U.S. responses to their initiatives. The PRC is unlikely to bow before U.S. demands, yet the character of the U.S. response, among other factors, will shape how the PRC and its companies behave in Latin America and the pace at which they proceed.

Such analysis is not intended to imply that the United States should initiate a new "Monroe Doctrine," telling the PRC to "stay out" of the region. Although such rhetoric might play well politically, and although it might induce China to proceed more cautiously in the short term, it would also work against U.S. strategic interests in the long term by strengthening the hand of more conservative forces in the PRC, and by fueling accusations in Latin America that its powerful neighbor to the north is "once again" trying to interfere with the sovereign right of countries in the region to maintain relations with whom they choose.

Beyond such a likely negative reaction from the region, trying to prevent the PRC from establishing military ties with Latin America would also deny the United States some of the real benefits that may be realized from Chinese military engagement with the region. To the extent that it proves reliable, for example, Chinese military hardware and supplies, in addition to training programs, may provide the region with cost-effective ways to meet security needs in the face of serious threats, such as those posed by transnational criminal organizations.[142] Cooperation between the PRC and Latin American police forces with data, personnel exchanges, and translation support, could be of great benefit in combating the activities of mafias operating in Latin America with ties to PRC criminal enterprises such as the Red Dragon, with its involvement in human trafficking networks in the region[143] — or in stemming the flow of precursor chemicals from China to cocaine laboratories in the Andes and Amazon jungle.[144] Revenue from export sales to China, if carefully managed, may also help Latin American states meet their security needs, as seen in the case of Chile, where by law, 10 percent of copper export revenues are channeled to fund defense modernization.[145]

Given both the positive and negative attributes of Chinese military engagement with the region, the United States should work to obtain greater transparency with regard to those activities, and to engage the PRC in a positive fashion regarding its pursuits in the hemisphere, including regular dialogue and the establishment of mechanisms for resolving misunderstanding. To this extent, the decision by U.S. Assistant Secretary of State Arturo Valenzuela to resume the U.S.-China Strategic Dialogue on Latin America[146] initiated by his predecessor, Thomas Shannon, was a constructive move.

As a complement to transparency, the United States must also improve its understanding of the dangers and the threats presented by that engagement in the specific, evolving Latin American context. Scenario-based gaming could play an important role in such analysis by generating insight with respect to how political crises and other potential future dynamics in the region could play out, with a particular focus on crises that threaten specific PRC interests in the region, and options for the PRC to protect those interests in unilateral as well as collaborative ways. Such analysis should also focus on how different actors in the region might react to the presence of China, including its indirectly applied pressures, and how the commercial and other interests in Latin America of such actors as Russia, Iran, and India might play into the unfolding dynamic.

Overall, it is important for the United States to forge its response to PRC military engagement with the region in strategic terms, considering both the long-term implications of Chinese actions, as well as how that response affects the U.S. position among the countries of the region. Chinese military engagement with Latin America is likely to be a growing and enduring part of the regional dynamic. How the United States adapts and reacts to that reality will have profound implications for the future security environment of the region, and the position of the United States within it.

ENDNOTES

1. "Full text: China's Policy Paper on Latin America and the Caribbean." *China View*, Beijing, China, November 5, 2008, available from *news.xinhuanet.com*.

2. For an example of the controversy, see "Panama Canal: America's strategic artery," *BBC News*, December 8, 1999, available from *news.bbc.co.uk*. See also Nelson Chung, "US faces surprise attack with canal giveaway: Analyst," *Global Security*, November 17, 1999, available from *www.globalsecurity.org*.

3. See, for example, Kevin P. Gallagher and Roberto Porzecanski, *The Dragon in the Room,* Stanford, CA: Stanford University Press, 2010.

4. See Murray Scott Tanner, "How China Manages Internal Security Challenges and Its Impact on PLA Missions," in Roy Kamphausen, David Lai, and Andrew Scobell, eds., *Beyond the Strait: PLA Missions Other than Taiwan*, Carlisle, PA: Strategic Studies Institute, U.S. Army War College, April, 2009, p. 52.

5. See "II. National Defense Policy," available from *www.china.org.cn/english/features/book/194485.htm*.

6. David Lai and Mark Miller, "Introduction," in Kamphausen, Lai, and Scobell, eds., *Beyond the Strait*, p. 16.

7. See, for example, Editorial, "On the PLA's Historical Mission in the New Stage of the New Century," *Jiefangjun Bao*, January 9, 2006. For references on calls for the PLA to create a "strategic deterrent force" to protect its interests abroad, see *PLA Daily* editorial, "On the Military's New Mission in the New Century," January 9, 2006. Also see Luo Yabo, "A Scientific Interpretation of the PLA's New Mission in the New Century," *Theoretical Studies on PLA Political Work*, Vol. 6, No. 3, June 2005. For a good overview of the debate over how the PLA should defend its interests abroad, see Lai and Miller, "Introduction," in Kamphausen, Lai, and Scobell, eds., *Beyond the Strait*.

8. "Petrolera china desestima que protesta en Tarapoa haya afectado sus intereses," *El Universo*, Guayaquil, Ecuador, November 16, 2006, available from *www.eluniverso.com*. See also "Andes Strikes Deal, Ends Tarapoa Protests," *Rigzone*, November 14, 2006, available from *www.rigzone.com/news/article.asp?a_id=38140*.

9. "Heridos 24 militares en incidentes en protestas en Orellana," *El Universo*, Guayaquil, Ecuador, July 5, 2007, available from *www.eluniverso.com*.

10. "Corredor logístico Manta-Manaos generará nuevas industrias locales," *El Universo*, Guayaquil, Ecuador, May 6, 2007, available from *www.eluniverso.com*.

11. "Los camioneros ratifican el boicot a los super y autoservicios chinos," *Clarin*, Buenos Aires, Argentina, June 26, 2006, available from *www.clarin.com*.

12. Yolanda Ojeda Reyes, "Ciudanos chinos reciben protección," *El Universal*, Caracas, Venezuela, November 11, 2004, available from *www.eluniversal.com*.

13. With global warming in the future, this could also include the Straits of Magellan.

14. Christopher D. Young and Ross Rustici, "China's Out of Area Naval Operations: Case Studies, Trajectories, Obstacles and Potential Solutions," *China Strategic Perspectives*, No. 3, Washington DC: National Defense University Press, December 2010.

15. Song Xiaojun, "Will China Send Forces to Somalia?" Blog commentary, December 1, 2008.

16. Lai and Miller, "Introduction," in Kamphausen, Lai, and Scobell, eds., *Beyond the Strait*.

17. Information Office of the State Council, *China's National Defense in 2008*, Beijing, China, available from *www.china.org.cn/government/central_government/2009-01/20/content_17155577.htm*. See also Information Office of the State Council, *China's National Defense in 2006,* Beijing, China, December 29, 2006.

18. For a good discussion of the Chinese approach towards "asymmetric warfare," see Nichalos R. Reisdorff, "Winning the Hundred Battles: China and Asymmetric Warfare," Master's Thesis, ADA430913, Ft. Leavenworth, KS: Army Command and General Staff College, June 6, 2003.

19. "Bolivia y China fortalecen cooperación militar," *Los Tiempos*, Cochabamba, Bolivia, August 18, 2010, available from *www.lostiempos.com*.

20. "Militares Cubanos Visitan China" ("Cuban Military Visits China"), *Cuba a la Mano*, September 4, 2010, available from *cubaalamano.net*.

21. "Saludan fortalecimiento de cooperación militar entre Fuerzas Armadas de Perú y China," *Andina*, Novembeer 23, 2010, available from *www.andina.com/pe*.

22. "China dona US$1 millón a Colombia para armamentos," *ABC*, Asunción, Paraguay, September 6, 2010, available from *www.abc.com.py*.

23. "Brazil seeks closer defense relationship with China: defense minister," *People's Daily Online*, Beijing, China, September 30, 2010, available from *english.people.com*.

24. "Chinese, Brazilian DMs hold talks on military cooperation," *People's Daily Online*, Beijing, China, September 9, 2010, available from *english.people.com*.

25. "Chinese military open to more int'l cooperation: senior officer," *People's Daily Online*, Beijing, China, September 15, 2010, available from *english.people.com.cn*.

26. "Ecuadoran defense minister meets with Chinese military delegation," *People's Daily Online*, Beijing, China, November 14, 2010, available from *english.people.com.cn*.

27. "Jefe del Estado Mayor chino está desde el martes en Venezuela," *El Universal*, Caracas, Venezuela, November 18, 2010, available from *www.eluniversal.com*.

28. "China confirms death of all 8 Chinese police officers in Haiti quake," *China View*, January 17, 2010, available from *www.chinaview.cn*. In the days following the earthquake, the PLA police contingent was temporarily augmented by rescue workers and other personnel from the PRC. "Chinese rescue team arrives in Haiti, eight Chinese still missing," *Peoples Daily Online*, Beijing, China, January 14, 2010, available from *english.people.com.cn*.

29. "Chinese rescue team arrives in Haiti, eight Chinese still missing." The official list of casualties associated with MINUSTAH, listing only four Chinese peacekeepers, can be found at MINUSTAH United Nations Stabilization Mission in Haiti, available from *www.un.org/en/peacekeeping/missions/minustah/memoriam.shtml*. An account of the collapse of the MINUSTAH headquarters can be found at "UN Headquarters in Haiti Collapsed in Quake," *CBS News*, January 13, 2009, available from *article.wn.com/view/2010/01/13/UN_Haiti_headquarter_collapses_in_earthquake/*.

30. "China further honors peacekeepers killed in Haiti earthquake," *Peoples Daily Online*, Beijing, China, January 26, 2010, available from *english.people.com.cn*.

31. See, for example, Florencia Jubany and Daniel Poon, "Recent Chinese Engagement in Latin America and the Caribbean: A Canadian Perspective," *FOCAL*, March 2006, available from *www.focal.ca/pdf/china_lat-am.pdf*.

32. There may be separate Air Force and Navy versions of this course.

33. The formal legal request to the Uruguayan Congress for the Naval Captain Sergio Dos Santos to attend the year-long course appears as Resolucion 56.547. Ministerio de Defensa Nacional. Ministerio de Relaciones Exteriores, Montevideo, Uruguay, April 29, 2009.

34. "Simpósio Internacional no Naval Command College do Exército Popular de Libertacão de China," *PlanoBrazil*, December 18, 2010.

35. "Curso de Chino Mandarín," *Ejército de Chile*, August 2, 2007, available from *www.ejercito.cl/detalle_noticia.php?noticia =3260*.

36. "China dona US$1 millón a Colombia para armamentos," *ABC*, Asunción, Paraguay, September 6, 2010, available from *www.abc.com.py*.

37. "Brazil seeks closer defense relationship with China: defense minister," *People's Daily Online*, Beijing, China, September 30, 2010, available from *english.people.com*.

38. Robert Benson, "Chinese Navy's Historic Pearl Harbor Visit," *Asia-Pacific Defense Forum*, Fall 1997, available from *forum. apan-info.net/fall_97/China_r.html*. See also Young and Rustici.

39. The ships in question left the Chinese port of Qingdao in October 2009, and completed their South American port calls in December 2009. "Dos buques militares chinos de última generación visitan Ecuador," *Observatorio de la política China*, December 12, 2009, available from *www.politica-china.org*.

40. One analysis notes that reports from past deployments suggest that issues such as repairing or replacing critical parts, and obtaining supplies such as fresh fruits and vegetables are critical obstacles for long-range force projection by the Chinese Navy. See Young and Rustici.

41. See, for example, "Chinese, Chilean navy commanders discuss ties," *China Daily*, Beijing, China, November 9, 2010, available from *chinadaily.com.cn/china/2010-11/09/content_11524530.htm*. See also "Hawaii to Host 10th Western Pacific Naval Symposium," U.S. Navy, October 29, 2006, available from *www.navy.mil/search/display.asp?story_id=26329*.

42. "Chinese honor guards shine at Mexico's independence parade," *People's Daily Online*, Beijing, China, September 19, 2010, available from *english.people.com.cn*.

43. "Ejércitos de Perú y China Concluyen operación de acción humanitaria conjunta en Lima," Andina, Peru, November 30, 2010, available from *www.andina.com.pe*.

44. "Operación Conjunta China-Peru de Rescate Medico Humanitario 'Angel de la Paz," *Maquina de Combate*, November 24, 2010, available from *maquina-de-combate.com/blog/archives/10429*.

45. "Ejercitos de Peru y China Popular culminan operación militar conjunta en salud," Andina, Peru, November 30, 2010, available from *www.andina.com.pe*.

46. Frank O. Mora, "Strategic Implications of China's Evolving Relationship with Latin America," Presentation to the Conference on China in Latin America, Washington DC, November 6, 2009, available from *www.ndu.edu/chds/China-Wksp/Presentations/CHDS-ChinaSpeech-Frank_Mora.pdf*.

47. Interview with General Carlos Ospina-Ovalle, Former Commander of the Colombian Armed Forces, Washington, DC, January 12, 2011, regarding his personal perspective on why Colombia had not purchased significant military end items from the PRC.

48. "Venezuela's Chavez to buy Chinese K-8 planes," *Reuters*, May 11, 2008, available from *www.reuters.com*.

49. "Venezuela Air Force to take delivery on Chinese jet trainer K-8 Karakorum next year," *World Military Forum*, November 28, 2009, available from *www.armybase.us/2009/11/venezuela-air-force-to-take-delivery-on-chinese-jet-trainer-k-8-karakorum-next-year/*.

50. "Aviación recibe primeros seis aviones chinos de combate K-8W," *El Universal*, Caracas, Venezuela, March 13, 2010, available from *www.el-universal.com*.

51. *Ibid*.

52. "En agosto llegan 12 nuevos aviones K-8," *El Universal*. Caracas, Venezuela, June 30, 2010, available from *www.el-universal.com*.

53. The possibility of purchasing the L-15 was discussed in meetings between the Chinese and Venezuelan military leadership in October 2009.

54. "Se cayó avión militar en Barquisimeto," *El Universal*, Caracas, Venezuela, July 21, 2010, available from *www.el-universal.com*.

55. "Venezuela compra a China 12 aviones de transporte," *El Universal*, Caracas, Venezuela, November 29, 2010, available from *www.el-universal.com*.

56. "Consideran comprar radares de baja cota," *El Universal*, Caracas, Venezuela, June 6, 2009, available from *www.el-universal.com*.

57. Maria Daniela Espanoza, "FAN utilizará radar de origen chino en ejercicio con Brasil," *El Universal*, Caracas, Venezuela, August 21, 2008, available from *www.el-universal.com*.

58. Noriega.

59. "Instalarán 10 radares chinos para mayor control del espacio aéreo," *El Universal*, Caracas, Venezuela, December 29, 2010, available from *www.el-universal.com*.

60. The JYL-1 radars purchased by Venezuela from the Chinese reportedly have an effective detection range of 240 nautical miles. For more information about the transaction, see "Consideran comprar radares de baja cota," *El Universal*, Caracas, Venezuela, June 6, 2009, available from *www.el-universal.com*.

61. Some confirmation of this activity appears in the resumes of Huawei personnel who mention having worked on the modernization of the DICOFAN network. See, for example, Monica Suinaga, Huawei Design Engineer, On-Line Resume, available from *ve.linkedin.com/pub/monica-suinaga/3/996/111.*

62. Huawei establece alianzas con el sector académico venezolano," *Caracas Digital,* January 24, 2011, available from *www.caracasdigital.com.*

63. "Colombia pide la captura de un diputado venezolano por 'Farcpolitica'," *El Tiempo,* December 5, 2009, available from *www.eltiempo.com;* See also "Fiscalía colombiana ordena detención de diputado venezolano Figueroa," *El Comercio,* Quito, Ecuador, December 6, 2009, available from *www.elcomercio.com.*

64. "Ecuador recibirá radares chinos para su frontera con Colombia," *El Universal,* Caracas, Venezuela, September 29, 2009, available from *www.el-universal.com.*

65. "Ecuador instalará cuatro radares en la frontera con Colombia este año," *El Universal,* Caracas, Venezuela, August 16, 2010, available from *www.el-universal.com.*

66. Interview with Guido Zambrano, Ministry of Transportation and Public Works, Quito, Ecuador, July 8, 2007.

67. "Ecuador negocia con China compra de aviones logísticos Javier Fernandez," *El Universo,* Guayaquil, Ecuador, July 30, 2009, available from *www.eluniverso.com.* See also "Ecuador comprará aviones a China, para reemplazar gran parte de su flota actual," *Aviación Argentina-over-blog,* July 30, 2009, available from *aviacionargentina.over-blog.com/article-34443350.html.*

68. "China Duplicará Colaboración Militar Copn Ecuador, Según Fuerzas Armadas Del Vecino País," *El Tiempo,* Bogota, Colombia, February 15, 2010, available from *www.eltiempo.com.*

69. "Ecuador comprará aviones de transporte militar chinos," *El Universo,* Guayaquil, Ecuador, August 16, 2010, available from *www.eluniverso.com.*

70. "Proyectos de la Fuerza Aerea Ecuatoriana," Saorbats, Ecuador, available from *www.saorbats.com.ar/news/1611*. See also "Ecuador comprará aviones de transporte militar chinos."

71. "China Duplicará Colaboración Militar Copn Ecuador."

72. "Bolivia comprará aviones chinos para lucha antidroga," *El Universo*, Guayaquil, Ecuador, October 2, 2009, available from *www.eluniverso.com*.

73. "Bolivia to receive combat aircraft from China," *Asia One*, January 19, 2011, available from *www.asiaone.com*.

74. "Gobierno ratifica compra de naves chinas y rusas," *Los Tiempos*, Cochabamba, Bolivia, January 15, 2010, available from *www.lostiempos.com*. See also "Bolivia to receive combat aircraft from China," *Asia One*, January 29, 2011, available from *www.asia-one.com*.

75. "El gobierno decide potenciar la fuerza aérea," *La Razón*, La Paz, Bolivia, February 19, 2007, available from *www.la-razon.com*. See also "La FAB se fortalece con un avión de carga," *La Razón*, La Paz, Bolivia, August 2, 2007, available from *www.la-razon.com*.

76. "In 2007, Bolivia sextuplico su deuda," *El Deber*, Santa Cruz, Bolivia, January 31, 2008, available from *www.eldeber.com.bo*.

77. "China dono equipos a las fuerzas armadas," *Los Tiempos*, Cochabamba, Bolivia, December 16, 2006, available from *www.lostiempos.com*.

78. "China regaló 43 vehiculos a las fuerzas armadas," *El Deber*, Santa Cruz, Bolivia, September 11, 2007, available from *www.eldeber.com.bo*.

79. "China donó a las FF.AA. de Bolivia US$2,6 millones," *AmericaEconomia*, March 31, 2010, available from *www.americaeconomia.com*.

80. "Bolivia y China fortalecen cooperación militar," *Los Tiempos*, Cochabamba, Bolivia, August 18, 2010, available from *www.lostiempos.com*.

81. "Bolivia aclara que 10.000 fusiles fueron donados por China y no por Venezuela," *Terra*, June 26, 2008, available from *noticias.terra.es*.

82. "Novedad en Parada Militar fue la presentación de cinco nuevos tanques chinos MBT 2000," *Agencia Peruana de Noticias*, December 8, 2009, available from *www.andina.com.pe*. See also "Tanques chinos: El Ejército está de acuerdo con la compra," *Peru21*, Lima, Peru, December 10, 2009, available from *peru21.com.pe*.

83. "El Ejecutivo busca postergar la compra de tanques chinos," *Gestion*, Lima, Peru, April 6, 2010, available from *gestion.pe/noticia/457657/ejecutivo-buscar-postergar-compra-tanques-chinos*.

84. "Perú y China firman un convenio de cooperación por 800 mil dólares," *El Comercio*, Lima, Peru, November 11, 2007, available from *www.elcomerciol.com.pe*.

85. Carlos Ospina-Ovalle. Former Commander-in-Chief of the Colombian Armed Forces, Interview, Washington, DC, December 1, 2009.

86. For photos of these cars in the colors of the municipal pólice of Montevideo, see "Geely Policía de Montevideo," *Flickr*, available from *www.flickr.com/photos/13328329@N06/4191019109/*.

87. "En el Perú ya se venden autos de la marca Geely," *El Comercio*, Lima, Peru, August 1, 2007, available from *www.elcomercio.com.pe*.

88. "China dona US$1 millón a Colombia para armamentos," *ABC*, Asuncion, Paraguay, September 6, 2010, available from *www.abc.com.py*.

89. "Costa Rica pidió a China Continental entrenamiento policial," *El Nuevo Diario*, Managua, Nicaragua, November 3, 2010, available from *www.elnuevodiario.com.ni*.

90. "Negocia la Argentina comprar helicópteros militares a China," *La Nación*, Buenos Aires, Argentina, May 17, 2007, available from *www.lanacion.com.ar*.

91. Guido Bratslavsky, "Licitación de radares: Ya hay trece empresas interesadas," *Clarín*, Buenos Aires, Argentina, January 29, 2007, available from *www.clarin.com*.

92. "Norinco Wmz-551b1 Ea," *Socyberty*, October 3, 2010, available from *socyberty.com/military/norinco-wmz-551b1-e*a.

93. Christian Vilada, "Argentina evalúa la adquisición de blindados chinos," *Saorbats*, August 27, 2008, available from *www.saorbats.com.ar/news/494*.

94. Jorge Elias, "Opinión: Llegaron los VCTP WMZ-551B1 chinos," *Desarrollo y Defensa*, September 10, 2010, available from *desarolloydefensa.blogspot.com*.

95. "Brazil seeks closer defense relationship with China: defense minister," *People's Daily Online*, Beijing, China, September 30, 2010, available from *english.people.com*.

96. "¿Privatización de Codelco? El rescate de los mineros pone en vitrina a la estatal," *AmericaEconomia*, December 12, 2010, available from *www.americaeconomia.co*m.

97. "China sends $3.5M in military equipment to Jamaica," *Today Online*, January 15, 2011, available from *www.todayonline.com*.

98. "Paraguay soldiers using Chinese M4 (CQ 5.56) carbines," *MilitaryPhotos.Net*, February 9, 2008, available from *www.military-photos.net/forums/showthread.php?141091-Paraguay-soldiers-using-Chinese-M4-(CQ-5.56)-rifles*.

99. *Firearms Trafficking: US efforts to face Arms Trafficking to Mexico Face Planning and Coordination Challenges*, GAO-09-709, Washington, DC: U.S. Government Accountability Office, June 2009.

100. Christopher Bodeen, "Future of Embraer China Plant Depends on Beijing," *ABC News*, November 17, 2010, available from *abcnews.go.com*. See also *Macauhub*, November 26, 2010, available from *Macau. www.macauhub.com.mo*. See also "Brazil's Embraer admits possibility of abandoning operations in China," *Macauhub*, Macau, Brazil, May 6, 2010, available from *www.macauhub.com.mo*.

101. "China invertirá 300 milliones de dólares en linea aerea venezolana," *El Universal*, Caracas, Venezuela, April 23, 2010, available from *www.el-universal.com*.

102. According to the agreement, within the umbrella of AVIC companies, two helicopters will be acquired from Changhe Aircraft Industries Group, while a total of 31 Y-12 fixed wing aircraft will be manufactured by Hafei Aviation Industry Co. Lan Lan and Mao Lijun, "AVIC Bags Big Deal in Venezuela," *China Daily*, July 13, 2010, available from *www.chinadaily.com.cn*.

103. Peter Ritter. "The New Space Race: China vs. US," *Time*, February 13, 2008, available from *www.time.com*.

104. In October 2007, China put an unmanned probe in orbit around the moon, and contemplates manned missions to the moon in the future. Jeffrey Logan, "China's Space Program: Options for U.S.-China Cooperation," Document RS22777, Washington, DC: Congressional Research Service, September 29, 2008.

105. Great Wall Industries, available from *www.cgwic.com*.

106. "Satellites: CBERS-1, 2 and 2B | CBERS-3 and 4," China-Brazil Earth Resources Satellite (CBERS), available from *www.cbers.inpe.br*.

107. "Chinese Space Policy: Collaboration or Competition," Washington, DC; Center for Strategic and International Studies, March 23, 2010, available from *csis.org*.

108. Fabíola de Olivera. *O Brasil Chega Ao Espaço: SCD-1 satélite de coleta de dados*, São José dos Campos, São Paolo, Brasil : Instituto Nacional de Pequisas Espaciais, 1996, p. 81.

109. "Hu Jintao Visits the China-Brazil Aeronautics and Space Cooperation Project in Sao Paulo," Beijing, China: Ministry of

Foreign Affairs of the People's Republic of China, November 15, 2004, available from *www.fmprc.gov.cn*.

110. De Olivera.

111. Gyanesh Chander, "An Overview of the CBERS-2 satellite and comparison of the CBERS-2 CCD data with the L5 TM data," Presentation, Washington, DC: U.S. Geological Survey, March 16, 2006.

112. Ironically, China and Brazil both ultimately joined the Missile Technology Control Regime. Luis Bitencourt, "Developing Countries and Missile Proliferation: The Cases of Argentina, Brazil and India," Ph.D. dissertation, Washington DC: Catholic University of America, 2001, p. 149.

113. "Brazil To Deepen Space Cooperation With China," *Space Daily*, March 27, 2008, available from *www.spacedaily.com*.

114. See R. Evan Ellis, "New Frontiers? China – Latin America Space Cooperation," *Security and Defense Studies Review*, Vol. 10, Spring-Summer 2010, p. 125.

115. "Chávez celebra satellite para construer el socalismo," *El Mercurio*, Santiago, Chile, October 30, 2008, available from *diario. elmercurio.cl*.

116. "Venezuela inicia operaciones del Satélite Simón Bolívar," *El Universal*, Caracas, Venezuela, January 10, 2009, available from *www.eluniversal.com*.

117. James Suggett, "Venezuela to Launch its First Satellite from China in November," *Venezuelanalysis*, August 18, 2008, available from *www.venezuelanalysis.com*.

118. "Bolivian, Chinese Tupac Katari Satellite Partnership Now Official," *Satellite Today*, April 6, 2010, available from *www. satellitetoday.com/civilspace/yheadlines/Bolivian-Chinese-Tupac-Katari-Satellite-Partnership-Now-Official_33806.html*.

119. "Bolivia firmó convenio con China para construcción de satélite Túpac Katari," *El Comercio*, Lima, Peru, April 1, 2010, available from *elcomercio.pe*.

120. "China aprueba crédito para satélite boliviano," *Los Tiempos*, La Paz, Bolivia, December 24, 2010, available from *www. lostiempos.com*.

121. "Venezuela CANTV Selected Huawei Technologies to Upgrade Its Optical Fiber National Backbone Network," Huawei, December 31, 2004, available from *www.huawei.com*.

122. Jamie Hulse, *China's Expansion into and U.S. Withdrawal from Argentina's Telecommunications and Space Industries and the Implications for U.S. National Security*, Carlisle, PA: Strategic Studies Institute, U.S. Army War College, September 2007.

123. "Arianespace Lands Arsat-1 Launch Contract," *Space-News*, June 28, 2010, available from *www.spacenews.com*.

124. "Defensa sondea 25 empresas para construir el nuevo satélite chileno," *El Mercurio*, Santiago, Chile, April 18, 2007, available from *diario.elmercurio.cl*.

125. "Astrium presents the completed SSOT satellite to the Chilean government," EADS Astrium, February 9, 2010, available from *www.astrium.eads.net/en/news/astrium-presents-the-completed-ssot-satellite-to-the-chilean-government.html*.

126. "Asia-Pacific Space Cooperation Organization starts operation," *China View*, December 16, 2008, available from *news.xinhuanet.com/english/2008-12/16/content_10514901.htm*.

127. Juan Arvizu and Horacio Jimenez, "Crean diputados agencia especial Mexicana," *El Universal*, Mexico City, Mexico, April 20, 2010, available from *www.eluniversal.com.mx*.

128. "Invitados," Conferencia Espacial de las Americas, available from *conferenciaespacialdelasamericas.org/agencias_espaciales.html*.

129. The projects are described in general terms in the the websites of both companies. See, for example, "Huawei America Latina," available from *www.huawei.com/es/catalog.do?id=343*. See also Hulse.

130. See, for example, Daniel Ricardo Hernandez, "Móvil bolivariano costar BsF 30," *El Universal*, Caracas, Venezuela, March 5, 2009, available from *www.el-universal.com*.

131. The 1,000-mile cable will extend from Camurey, Venezuela, to Siboney, Cuba, and is expected to be functional in July 2011. "Cuba, Venezuela Link Via Undersea Cable," *The Right Perspective*, January 23, 2011, available from *www.therightperspective. org*.

132. "Preocupados trabajadores por possible privatizacion de Hondutel," *La Tribuna*, Tegucigalpa, Honduras, October 23, 2010, available from *www.latribuna.com*.

133. Jia Wen. "Remembering Chinese peacekeepers in Haiti," *Global Times*, January 19, 2010, available from *opinion.globaltimes. cn/observer/2010-01/499318.html*.

134. Manuel Cereijo, "Inside Bejucal Base in Cuba: A Real Threat," *The Americano*, August 27, 2010, available from *theamericano.com/2010/08/27/bejucal-base-cuba-real-threat/*. Cereijo's allegations concerning Bejucal, however, have been questioned by Cuban scholar William Ratliff, among others, noting that the radar domes in the photo accompanying Cereijo's article are not located at Bejucal, as represented, but rather, the U.S.-operated Menwith Hill facility in the United Kingdom. See "Cereijo, Bejucal, China and Cuba's adversary foreign intelligence (Bill Ratliff, US)," Stanford, CA: World Association of International Studies, Stanford University, April 3, 2006, available from *waisworld.org/go.jsp?id=0 2a0&objectType=post&objectTypeId=3776&topicId=10*.

135. "Chinese Signals Intelligence and Cyberwarfare in Cuba," *AFIO Weekly Intelligence Notes*, No. 23-06, June 12, 2006, available from *www.afio.com/sections/wins/2006/2006-23.html#ChinaInCuba*.

136. "China begins 26th Antarctica season with a team of 251 scientists," *Mercopress*, October 14, 2009, available from *en.mercopress.com/2009/10/13/china-begins-26th-antarctica-season-with-a-team-of-251-scientists*.

137. Young and Rustici.

138. "China bolsters Antarctica posts," *BBC News*, November 6, 2007, available from *news.bbc.co.uk/2/hi/asia-pacific/7080888.stm*.

139. Andrew Darby, "China flags its Antarctic intent," *The Sidney Morning Herald*, January 11, 2010, available from *www.smh.com. au/opinion/politics/china-flags-its-antarctic-intent-20100111-m287. html*.

140. Young and Rustici.

141. J. Michael Waller, "China's Beachhead at Panama Canal," *BNet*, August 16, 1999, available from *findarticles.com/p/articles/mi_m1571/is_30_15/ai_55481519/*.

142. A similar argument was made by Deputy Assistant Secretary of Defense Frank O. Mora, "Strategic Implications of China's Evolving Relationship with Latin America," Presentation to the Conference on China in Latin America, Washington, DC, November 6, 2009, available from *www.ndu.edu/chds/China-Wksp/ Presentations/CHDS-ChinaSpeech-Frank_Mora.pdf*.

143. José Melendez, "La mafia china aumenta el tráfico de personas en AL," *El Universal*, Mexico City, Mexico, May 10, 2007, available from *www.eluniversal.com.mx*.

144. "China Tightens Restrictions on Online Transactions of Drug Precursor Chemicals," *Xinhua*, September 27, 2010, available from *english.cri.cn/6909/2010/09/27/45s596567.htm*.

145. See, for example, Daisy Johnson, "Developments regarding the Copper Reserve Fund in the Chilean Defence Funding Strategy," *Defense Viewpoints*, January 21, 2011, available from *www.defenceviewpoints.co.uk/articles-and-analysis/developments-regarding-the-copper-reserve-fund-in-the-chilean-defence-funding-strategy*.

146. "Assistant Secretary Valenzuela's Travel to China," U.S. Department of State, August 12, 2010, available from *www.state. gov/r/pa/prs/ps/2010/08/145941.htm*.

www.ingramcontent.com/pod-product-compliance
Lightning Source LLC
Chambersburg PA
CBHW072343290526
45794CB00002B/1002